The Poetry Show 2

David Orme and James Sale
Directors of the Schools' Poetry Association

MACMILLAN
EDUCATION

First published 1987

Published by
MACMILLAN EDUCATION LTD
Houndmills, Basingstoke, Hampshire RG21 2XS
and London
Companies and representatives
throughout the world

Designed by Linda Reed

Illustrated by David Eyre

Printed in Hong Kong

British Library Cataloguing in Publication Data
Orme, David
The poetry show.
2
1. Poetics
I. Title   II. Sale, James
808.1   PN1042
ISBN 0–333–39786–X

Contents

Acknowledgements

The editors and publishers wish to thank the following who have kindly given permission for the use of copyright material:

Carcanet Press Limited for 'Anger lay by me all night long', from *Collected Poems* by Elizabeth Daryush;
Kathleen Raine for 'Amo Ergo Sum';
Oxford University Press for 'To Curse Her', from *The Complete Poems of Keith Douglas* edited by Desmond Graham, © Marie J. Douglas 1978 (21 lines);
James Kirkup for 'Undivided Loyalty', from *The Prodigal Son*;
Jonathan Cape Ltd and the Estate of Robert Frost for 'Stopping by Woods on a Snowy Evening' and 'Nothing Gold Can Stay', from *The Poetry of Robert Frost* edited by Edward Connery Lathem;
David Horner for 'Poetree';
Editions Gallimard for 'Il Pleut', from *Calligrammes* by Guillaume Apollinaire, © Editions Gallimard 1925;
John Whalley for 'The Difference';
Gwen Dunn for 'Flo, the White Duck';
David Higham Associates Limited for 'Cat!', from *Silver Sand and Snow* by Eleanor Farjeon;
Laurence Pollinger Ltd for 'Piazza Piece', from *Selected Poems* by John Crowe Ransom, first published by Methuen London Ltd; Laurence Pollinger Ltd for 'A Sort of a Song', from *The Collected Earlier Poems of William Carlos Williams*;
Faber and Faber Publishers for 'My Papa's Waltz', from *The Collected Poems of Theodore Roethke*;
David Higham Associates Ltd for 'Death of an Aircraft', from *Collected Poems* by Charles Causley (65 lines);
Andre Deutsch for 'The Three Winds', from *Selected Poems* by Laurie Lee;
Faber and Faber Publishers for 'Swifts', from *Season Songs* by Ted Hughes;
Chatto & Windus for 'Pigeons', from *Differences* by Richard Kell;
Hippopotamus Press for 'Millipede' by Roy Bennett;
Wes Magee for 'Sheep, Buried';
Vernon Scannell for 'Mastering the Craft';
Gerald Duckworth & Co Ltd for 'Winter the Huntsman', from *Selected Poems* by Osbert Sitwell (20 lines);
Maurice Michael for 'With People, So With Trees' by Mervyn Peake;
Carcanet Press Limited for 'Winter Warfare', from *Behind the Eyes* by Edgell Rickword, © Estate of Edgell Rickword 1976 (20 lines);
Penguin Books Ltd for 'When it is the earth I tread . . .', from *The Earliest English Poems*, translated and introduced by Michael Alexander (Penguin Classics 1966, second edition 1977, p. 94 © Michael Alexander, 1966, 1977);
Jim C. Wilson for 'The Last Lie';
Century Hutchinson Publishing Group Ltd for 'To a Lady seen from a Train', from *Collected Poems* by Frances Cornford;
Gavin Ewart for 'The War Game' which appeared in AMBIT, © Gavin Ewart;
Anthony Sheil Associates Ltd for 'The Drawer', 'The Compasses', 'Owl' and 'A Child's Garden' by George MacBeth;
Secker & Warburg for 'The Day the World Ended' and 'A Poem for Breathing', from *Poems of Love and Death* and 'One Gone, Eight to Go' from *Poems from Oby* by George MacBeth.

The editors and publishers wish to acknowledge the following photograph sources:

Arvon Foundation, p. 62; Terry Banner, p. 82; Gary Boswell, p. 27, 75, 76; J. Allan Cash Ltd, p. 79, Arthur Guinness Son and Company (Great Britain) Limited, p. 29.

Every effort has been made to trace all the copyright holders, but if any have been inadvertently overlooked the publishers will be pleased to make the necessary arrangements at the first opportunity.

Preface

Lewis Carroll writes:

> For first you write a sentence,
> And then you chop it small;
> Then mix the bits, and sort them out
> Just as they chance to fall:
> The order of the phrases makes
> No difference at all.

The Poetry Show is an attempt to show pupils and teachers just how poetry is written. For poetry is not a result of chance, but of skilful craftsmanship, and the order of the phrases makes every difference in the world.

Simply used as an anthology, *The Poetry Show* provides ample and varied poetry material. The familiar and less well-known, modern and past, accessible and more challenging sorts of poetry fill these pages. However, *The Poetry Show* is far more than an anthology: it is a systematic effort to explain poetry, to demonstrate poetry's techniques, to raise questions for class discussion, to point the directions towards profitable class and individual work. There is here abundant material to read, to discuss, to work with.

The Poetry Show series follows a common pattern: six chapters – Introduction, Rhythm/Form, Rhyme/Sound, Words, Imagery, Drafting/The Living Poet. This is to concentrate attention on the specific features of poetry. Within these chapters the pattern tends to be three or four short units where narrative text is interspersed with

- ■ Discussion material
  and
- □ Work suggestions

Ideas are introduced sequentially, but these books are ideal for dipping into: even the non-specialist teacher could confidently teach a lesson, say on personification from Chapter 5, and any pupil should understand iambic metre from the clear explanation and lively illustrations in Chapter 2.

A special feature is the emphasis on living poets: these are introduced in the last chapter of each book, where their particular techniques of writing are fully examined.

In addition to the work suggestions within each chapter, the first five chapters are followed by 'Endpieces' – projects designed to involve the whole class in a range of varied and interesting poetry activities.

In short these books help teachers cover every aspect of poetry suitable for pupils from Middle School to GCSE level, providing a visually and intellectually stimulating challenge to pupils.

Some will doubtless argue that we 'murder to dissect' and that in analysing the techniques of poetry we are spoiling the poem. The confusion here is largely one of terminology. We do not advocate 'taking a poem to bits' or treating poetry as an object for comprehension exercises. On the contrary, we believe that a full appreciation of poetry comes from looking at it closely. The alternative is casual acquaintance, and how can this be said to heighten the experience of reading and writing poetry?

As Directors of the Schools' Poetry Association we have been increasingly confronted by teachers requesting more information on the technical aspects of writing, and how to present this kind of material to students. We believe that *The Poetry Show* goes a long way towards meeting such requests. We also believe that the move towards writing as a craft-based activity is the way forward for poetry teaching in our schools.

David Orme
James Sale

Comparisons

1 Questions

What questions do you find you want to ask about a poem? And suppose you have two similar poems: how can you compare them?

☐ First we should look for the most obvious things: list the questions you would ask about a poem and its author. Now look at *Nikki-Rosa*:

Nikki-Rosa

childhood remembrances are always a drag
if you're Black
you always remember things like living in Woodlawn
with no inside toilet
and if you become famous or something
they never talk about how happy you were to have your mother
all to yourself and
how good the water felt when you got your bath from one of those
big tubs that folk in chicago barbecue in
and somehow when you talk about home
it never gets across how much you
understood their feelings
as the whole family attended meetings about Hollydale
and even though you remember
your biographers never understand
your father's pain as he sells his stock
and another dream goes
and though you're poor it isn't poverty that
concerns you
and though they fought a lot
it isn't your father's drinking that makes any difference
but only that everybody is together and you
and your sister have happy birthdays and very good christmasses
and I really hope no white person ever has cause to write about me
because they never understand Black love is Black wealth and they'll
probably talk about my hard childhood and never understand that
all the while I was quite happy

NIKKI GIOVANNI (1943–   )

Study this chart, and write down the letter of the box you think contains the answer to each question:

Nikki-Rosa

Questions	Possible answers			
	A	B	C	D
1 Written by	man	woman	child	computer
2 Author is	white	black	oriental	green extra terrestial
3 Country of origin	UK	USA	USSR	Lapland
4 Century of origin	19th	20th	18th	4004 BC
5 Form of poem is	shape poem	freely written	stanzaic	syllabic
6 Subject	daffodils	a Black person	mermaids	lollipops
7 Theme	love	family life	war	death

In order to decide which are the answers we need evidence.

■ What evidence is there that the country of origin is the USA? We need to look at the words in the poem very closely.

■ We see that Nikki Giovanni was born in 1943, and so the poem must be 20th-century. But even if we didn't see 1943, there is evidence within the poem that it is 20th-century. Black 'consciousness' is a 20th-century movement: what line speaks most of Black awareness?

Nikki Giovanni's poem begins
      childhood remembrances are always a drag
and ends
      all the while I was quite happy

☐ Quite a change. Write a poem with lines of different lengths, as in *Nikki-Rosa*, using the same opening and closing lines.

The correct answers to *Nikki-Rosa* are all in column *B*.
☐ Now copy out a second table of questions. Read this poem and complete the details.

Little Black Boy

My mother bore me in the southern wild,
And I am black, but O! my soul is white;
White as an angel is the English child,
But I am black, as if bereav'd of light.

My mother taught me underneath a tree,
And sitting down before the heat of day
She took me on her lap and kissed me,
And pointing to the east, began to say:

'Look on the rising sun! there God does live,
And gives his light and gives his heat away;
And flowers and trees and beasts and men receive
Comfort in morning, joy in the noon day.

'And we are put on earth a little space
That we may learn to bear the beams of love;
And these black bodies and this sun-burnt face
Is but a cloud, and like a shady grove;

'For when our souls have learn'd the heat to bear,
The cloud will vanish: we shall hear his voice,
Saying: "come out from the grove, my love & care,
And round my golden tent like lambs rejoice."'

Thus did my mother say, and kissed me.
And thus I say to little English boy:
When I from black and he from white cloud free
And round the tent of God like lambs we joy,

I'll shade him from the heat, till he can bear
To lean in joy upon our father's knee;
And then I'll stand and stroke his silver hair,
And be like him, and he will then love me.

WILLIAM BLAKE (1757–1827)

You will notice that your answers for the *Little Black Boy* are very different from those for *Nikki-Rosa*. Perhaps only the subject remains the same: a Black person.

2 Emotions

Our last two poems dealt with the topic of being Black. Strong emotions were expressed. Often poets want to express just their emotions – they want to say how they feel.

William Blake was a White man, but he sympathized with the Black boy. Nikki Giovanni is a Black woman and writes about her Black past.

■ Which poem is more personal? Which is more sincere? Which has most feeling? Discuss your answers.

■ What emotions and feelings do you have? Which are positive ones, and which negative? List them:

positive	negative
sincerity	jealousy
hope	hate
. . .	. . .

Here are two very different emotions being presented:

Anger lay by me all night long

Anger lay by me all night long,
  His breath was hot upon my brow,
He told me of my burning wrong,
  All night he talked and would not go.

He stood by me all through the day,
  Struck from my hand the book, the pen;
He said: 'Hear first what I've to say,
  And sing, if you've the heart to, then.'

And can I cast him from my couch?
  And can I lock him from my room?
Ah no, his honest words are such
  That he's my true-lord, and my doom.

ELIZABETH DARYUSH (1887–1977)

Amo Ergo Sum

Because I love
   The sun pours out its rays of living gold
   Pours out its gold and silver on the sea.

Because I love
   The earth upon her astral spindle winds
   Her ecstasy-producing dance.

Because I love
   Clouds travel on the winds through wide skies,
   Skies wide and beautiful, blue and deep.

Because I love
   Wind blows white sails,
   The wind blows over flowers, the sweet wind blows.

Because I love
   The ferns grow green, and green the grass, and green
   The transparent sunlit trees.

Because I love
   Larks rise up from the grass
   And all the leaves are full of singing birds.

Because I love
   The summer air quivers with a thousand wings,
   Myriads of jewelled eyes burn in the light.

Because I love
   The iridescent shells upon the sand
   Take forms as fine and intricate as thought.

Because I love
   There is an invisible way across the sky,
   Birds travel by that way, the sun and moon
   And all the stars travel that path by night.

Because I love
   There is a river flowing all night long.

Because I love
   All night the river flows into my sleep,
   Ten thousand living things are sleeping in my arms,
   And sleeping wake, and flowing are at rest.

KATHLEEN RAINE (1908–   )

In the first poem, anger is like someone next to the poet, controlling her future – a future of doom. She tries to read, she tries to write, but Anger, her 'true-lord', prevents all this. 'He' reminds her of her 'burning wrong'.

■ Isn't this like anger – we think of wrong done to us by someone?

Amo Ergo Sum means 'I love therefore I am'. There is no anger in this poem, only love. Because the poet loves, all nature – the sun, the earth, the grass, the birds, the rivers – seems radiant and at rest. Everything seems happy and relaxed.

■ Isn't this like love – when we're in love we think how wonderful the world is?

□ Now use some of the emotion words from your list. Substitute your words for 'Anger' and 'love' in the two poems. Do the new words fit the rest of the poem? For example,

    Jealousy lay by me all night long

or

    Because I hate

Rewrite one poem to suit your new opening line.

■ Different emotions – and two poems of very different shapes. What differences of shape are there? Discuss these. Notice rhymes and word repetitions. Do you think the shape of the poems suitable to the emotions described?

□ Choose one of the emotions from the list, and write your own poem:

    Because I . . .

Try to describe exactly how that emotion *feels*.

3 Contrasts

Some people think poetry is only about daffodils and nature. Of course this is wrong. Poetry usually deals with subjects that concern *us*.

■ What subjects do you think are important?

□ Make a list of the six most important topics in the world.

We think such a list is bound to include some of these: religious beliefs, worship, morals, principles, relationships, family, marriage, love, sex, environment, nature, pollution, creatures, war, holocaust, torture, death, horror.

    The trouble is, everyone has their own opinion. Poets are no exception. And poetry reflects all these different views. Our first section showed two very different poets defending Black people. The second section showed two different emotions being described.

Now here are two contrasting attitudes to the Christian religion:

The Grey Squirrel

Like a small grey
coffee-pot,
sits the squirrel.
He is not

all he should be,
kills by dozens
trees, and eats
his red-brown cousins.

The keeper on the
other hand,
who shot him, is
a Christian, and

loves his enemies,
which shows
the squirrel was not
one of those.

HUMBERT WOLFE (1885–1940)

The Donkey

When fishes flew and forests walked
    And figs grew upon thorn,
Some moment when the moon was blood,
    Then surely I was born;

With monstrous head and sickening cry
    And ears like errant wings,
The devil's walking parody
    On all four-footed things.

The tattered outlaw of the earth,
    Of ancient crooked will;
Starve, scourge, deride me: I am dumb,
    I keep my secret still.

Fools! For I also had my hour;
    One far fierce hour and sweet:
There was a shout about my ears,
    And palms before my feet!

G.K. CHESTERTON (1874–1936)

■ These poems have much in common. What? Look at the number
of stanzas and lines. How are the rhymes arranged? What about
the titles? Which character is connected with the squirrel? And
which with the donkey?

☐ Use the chart on page 2 and complete it for both poems.

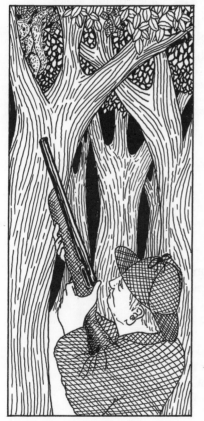 

Keeper *shoots* squirrel   Christ *rides* donkey
'means'   'means'
Christians are hypocrites   Monstrosities are glorious

The pattern is the same in both poems: some action by a person gives
special meaning to the animal.

We often think creatures have human thoughts and feelings.

> A fox is sly
> A tortoise is patient
> A cat is ?

☐ Make a list of creatures. Write down what you think they are like.

■ Discuss your choice of adjectives.

☐ Pick one creature from your list. Write a short poem about the creature. Introduce some human who does something to it or with it. Try to make a point about a cause or issue you feel strongly about.

☐ Organise a debate between two groups, representing 'the Squirrel' and 'the Donkey'. Here are some possible topics:

This House believes that religion is good for the world
This House believes that blood sports should be abolished
This House believes that killing is wrong in all circumstances

---

ANTHOLOGY 1

Break, Break, Break

Break, break, break,
  On thy cold gray stones, O Sea!
And I would that my tongue could utter
  The thoughts that arise in me.

O well for the fisherman's boy,
  That he shouts with his sister at play!
O well for the sailor lad,
  That he sings in his boat on the bay!

And the stately ships go on
  To their haven under the hill;
But O for the touch of a vanish'd hand,
  And the sound of a voice that is still!

Break, break, break,
  At the foot of thy crags, O Sea!
But the tender grace of a day that is dead
  Will never come back to me.

LORD TENNYSON

Là, tout n'est qu'ordre et beauté,
Luxe, calme, et volupté.

Anguilla, Adina,
Antigua, Cannelles,
Andreuille, all the I's,
Voyelles, of the liquid Antilles,
The names tremble like needles
Of anchored frigates,
Yachts tranquil as lilies,
In ports of calm coral,
The lithe, ebony hulls
Of strait-stitching schooners,
The needles of their masts
That thread archipelagoes
Refracted embroidery
In feverish waters
Of the sea-farer's islands,
Their shorn, leaning palms,
Shaft of Odysseus,
Cyclopic volcanoes,
Creak their own histories,
In the peace of green anchorage;
Flight, and Phyllis,
Returned from the Grenadines,
Names entered this sabbath,
In the port-clerk's register;
Their baptismal names,
The sea's liquid letters,
Repos donnez a cils . . .
And their blazing cargoes
Of charcoal and oranges;
Quiet, the fury of their ropes.
Daybreak is breaking
On the green chrome water,
The white herons of yachts
Are at sabbath communion,
The histories of schooners
Are murmured in coral,
Their cargoes of sponges
On sandspits of islets
Barques white as white salt
Of acrid Saint Maarten,
Hulls crusted with barnacles,

Holds foul with great turtles,
Whose ship-boys have seen
The blue heave of Leviathan,
A sea-faring, Christian,
And intrepid people.

Now an apprentice washes his cheeks
With salt water and sunlight.

In the middle of the harbour
A fish breaks the Sabbath
With a silvery leap.
The scales fall from him
In a tinkle of church-bells;
The town streets are orange
With the week-ripened sunlight,
Balanced on the bowsprit
A young sailor is playing
His grandfather's chantey
On a trembling mouth-organ.
The music curls, dwindling
Like smoke from blue galleys,
To dissolve near the mountains.
The music uncurls with
The soft vowels of inlets,
The christening of vessels,
The titles of portages,
The colours of sea-grapes,
The tartness of sea-almonds,
The alphabet of church-bells,
The peace of white horses,
The pastures of ports,
The litany of islands,
The rosary of archipelagoes,
Anguilla, Antigua,
Virgin of Guadeloupe,
And stone-white Grenada
Of sunlight and pigeons,
The amen of calm waters,
The amen of calm waters,
The amen of calm waters.

DEREK WALCOTT

Nothing is worth dying for.
Some people would rather
Be dead than Red.
But I would simply rather
Not be dead.

I would not die for Britain
Or any land. Why should I?
I only happened to be born there.
Emigré, banished, why should I defend
A land I never chose, that never wanted me?

I might have been born anywhere —
In mid-Pacific or in Ecuador.
I would not die for the world.
Jesus was wrong.
Only nothing is worth dying for.

JAMES KIRKUP

To Lucasta, on Going to the Wars

Tell me not, Sweet, I am unkind
   That from the nunnery
Of thy chaste breast and quiet mind,
   To war and arms I fly.

True, a new mistress now I chase,
   The first foe in the field;
And with a stronger faith embrace
   A sword, a horse, a shield.

Yet this inconstancy is such
   As you too shall adore;
I could not love thee, dear, so much,
   Loved I not honour more.

RICHARD LOVELACE

My Luve

O my Luve is like a red, red rose,
 That's newly sprung in June:
O my Luve is like the melodie,
 That's sweetly played in tune.

As fair art thou, my bonnie lass,
 So deep in luve am I;
And I will luve thee still, my dear,
 Till a' the seas gang dry.

Till a' the seas gang dry, my dear,
 And the rocks melt wi' the sun;
And I will luve thee still, my dear,
 While the sands o' life shall run.

And fare-thee-weel, my only Luve!
 And fare-thee-weel a while!
And I will come again, my Luve,
 Tho' it were ten thousand mile.

ROBERT BURNS

To Curse Her

You're handsome and false, and I could cover
that face with praise till I've stretched over
a figurative mask of words
for beauty; or my pen unloads
all that's packed up in the mind.
Then call a truce, and never find
enough, you are so fair, to do you honour.

The only voice to put with yours
Ulysses heard and strained the hawse
till it scarce held him to the sane mast –
I think your hair so glistened last
when Troilus found you in your uncle's hall,
jettisoned his arms with a humble gesture, fell
conquered, poor hero, in a deceitful house.

And if to portray you will exhaust
legends, illusion, eloquence, what most
will abash all my ingenuity
is doing justice to your perfidy.
Cressida could not match you, but I pray
you'll feel Cressida's ruin and decay
known for a strumpet, diseased and outcast.

KEITH DOUGLAS

ENDPIECE: Contrasts

This chapter has dealt with the contrasting attitudes, emotions, and beliefs of different poems. We have done this by considering two poems together.

- ☐ Search through this book and choose one poem you particularly like. Prepare a talk for your class on it.
- – Start with some background information – if you can find it – on the poet: the sort of questions you might answer might be those listed on page 2. Any others?
- – Discuss the features of the poem you like: the subject? the theme? the language? the atmosphere? something else?

- ☐ Tape your talk – it could form part of a class tape library of talks on poems.

- ☐ Use the poem as a starting point for your own new poem. Try to write a piece that contrasts with your original.

Beat-Up

1 Shape Poems

In Book 1 we looked at shape-words and shape-sentences. Now *shape-poems*:

Easter Wings

Lord, who createdst man in wealth and store,
Though foolishly he lost the same,
Decaying more and more,
Till he became
Most poor:
With thee
O let me rise
As larks, harmoniously,
And sing this day thy victories:
Then shall the fall further the flight in me.

GEORGE HERBERT

■ The title of this poem helps us understand it. What does the shape resemble? Can you think of any reason why Herbert chose it? And why *wings*? What does Easter stand for?

☐ Now attempt your own poem to match Herbert's: *Good Friday*. What shape might you 'hang' your poem on?

Easter Wings and *Good Friday* have simple shapes. A more difficult shape-poem could be written about:

a fire   a tree   a river   a car

☐ Create a shape-poem called *It's Raining*, then compare your version with Apollinaire's in the collection at the end of this chapter.

2 Beat-up

SEE ──────→ PATTERNS
HEAR ──────→ RHYTHMS (a pattern in sound)

The secret of finding rhythm is to listen. When a rhythm is regular it is called *metre*. Find your pulse: it beats – up and down.

Think of waves of blood! When you feel the strong beat (or throb), the wave is rising high. Then it crashes down, until the next wave.

■ Can you see the wave in two ways? Either up first and down after:

Or down first and up after:

☐ Listen: Arise.
　　　Falling.
　　Say these words aloud. Now say them again:
　　　　arise, arise, arise, arise, arise
　　　　falling, falling, falling, falling, falling

■ Which word has the beat-up on the first syllable, and the beat-down on the second? The other word has the pattern (rhythm) reversed. Can you hear the difference?

Suppose we mark the *beat-up* as '/' and the *beat-down* as 'x'.

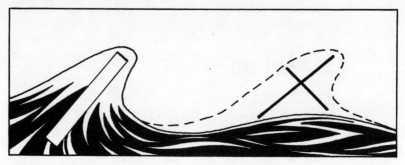

'Arise' would be

        x /
        arise

and if it were two words

        x /
        a rise

or

        x   /
        the rise

The second syllable would still have the beat.

☐ Here are ten words of two syllables each. Each syllable is either 'beat-up' or 'beat-down'. Mark them for beat. Two are done for you.

  /   x
village   stopping   farmhouse   between   frozen   darkest

                x /
harness   mistake   only   before

■ Are most two-syllable words like this 'x/' or this '/x'? Think of other two-syllable words.

☐ Read this poem carefully and slowly. It is divided into four parts: these are called *stanzas*.

Stopping by Woods on a Snowy Evening

Whose woods these are I think I know,
His house is in the village though;
He will not see me stopping here
To watch his woods fill up with snow.

My little horse must think it queer
To stop without a farmhouse near
Between the woods and frozen lake
The darkest evening of the year.

He gives his harness bells a shake
To ask if there is some mistake.
The only other sound's the sweep
Of easy wind and downy flake.

The woods are lovely, dark and deep,
But I have promises to keep,
And miles to go before I sleep,
And miles to go before I sleep.

ROBERT FROST

☐ Copy out some of this poem, marking it for its beat (using '/' and 'x').

■ What do you notice about the rhythm? Re-read the poem if you
are not sure. Does it follow a pattern? A metre? If so, what is it? Do
the lines begin beat-up first or beat-down?

Once you hear the metre, you want to keep it in all the lines to
come! The 'x/'pattern is called *iambic*.

☐ Make a list of one- and two-syllable words. Start connecting them
in sentences, trying to keep the iambic metre. For example:

    x /   x   / x / x   /
    a sentence is a list of words

    x / x   /   x /   x /
    I'm trying hard to keep in shape . . .

You will see our lines have four beat-ups: the same number as
Stopping by Woods.

If you have any doubts about whether your lines are iambic, compare
them with these lines:

As I was going up the stair
I met a man who wasn't there.
He wasn't there again today;
I wish, I wish he'd stay away.

HUGHES MEARNS

You may use this as a pattern for your iambic metre.

3 Beat Feet

We count the number of syllables in a line: we measure the metre.
We said *Stopping by Woods on a Snowy Evening* has four beat-ups –
four *feet*.

      x/   = 1 iambic foot
      x/x/ = 2 iambic feet

and so on. One iambic foot contains two syllables: unstressed,
stressed.

■ How many feet per line does this poem have?

Upon His Departure Hence

Thus I
Pass by
And die:
As One,
Unknown,
And gone:
A shade,
And laid
I' th' grave:
There have
My cave.
Where tell
I dwell,
Farewell.

ROBERT HERRICK

☐ Use Robert Herrick's *Thus I* as a model for your own poem. Look
   closely: two syllables for each line, and the beat on the second
   syllable. Try a poem beginning
      Thus you
  or
      Thus he
  or
      Thus she
   and make your last line
      Hello

One foot ————→ monometer
Two feet ————→ dimeter
Three feet ————→ trimeter
Four feet ————→ tetrameter

can see, this is a very short line!

■ Do you think there is any connection between the shortness of the line and the subject of the poem, how swiftly life is over? What effect does jumping from line to line so quickly have?

The choice of line length is important. Different lengths can be used for different effects. The monometer is too short for most purposes.

■ Look at *The Eagle and the Mole* and discuss, as you read through it, the following questions: What metre is it? How many feet are there in each line? So what sort of line is it? And how many stanzas are there in the poem?

The Eagle and the Mole

Avoid the reeking herd,
Shun the polluted flock,
Live like that stoic bird,
The eagle of the rock.

The huddled warmth of crowds
Begets and fosters hate;
He keeps, above the clouds,
His cliff inviolate.

When flocks are folded warm,
And herds to shelter run,
He sails above the storm,
He stares into the sun.

If in the eagle's track
Your sinews cannot leap,
Avoid the lathered pack,
Turn from the steaming sheep.

If you would keep your soul
From spotted sight or sound,
Live like the velvet mole;
Go burrow underground.

And there hold intercourse
With roots of trees and stones,
With rivers at their source,
And disembodied bones.

ELINOR WYLIE

The lines are iambic trimeters – three feet in each line. Like the
Herrick poem, the lines seem short and abrupt. Many begin with a
single word of command: 'Avoid', 'Shun', 'Live'. No wonder the
poem seems clipped and direct. But notice, too, that the iambic
pattern is sometimes broken:

    x / x / x   /
    Avoid the reeking herd,

    / x   x / x   /
    Shun the polluted flock,

This prevents monotony: but the metre is still iambic.

■ How many other lines can you spot where the iambic foot, x /, is
reversed to / x?

□ *The Eagle and the Mole* presents two creatures living at opposite
extremes – above and below, far-sighted and short-sighted, bird
and animal. Choose two creatures that you think are very
different. Write a poem recommending them.

□ Here is an iambic trimeter:

    Alone he rides, alone

Now add three more lines in the same metre and measure.
Compare your poem with *By the Statue of King Charles at Charing
Cross* (page 25).

LITTLE ACORNS

if the oaks tell jokes
if the palm can sing a psalm
if the elm excels at villanelles
if the ash can bash out a sonnet
if the sycamore cares for metaphor
if the weeping-willow trees like similes
if the chestnut's nuts about raps and chants
if the pines and the limes write lines that rhyme
if the hickory's trick is the limerick
if the yew does a cool haiku or clerihew
if the plane can scribble a cinquain
if the apple counts in syllables
if the firs prefer free verse
if the plum makes puns

THEN
LET
THIS
BE MY
POE T REE

DAVID HORNER

listen to the fall of all the perpendiculars of your existence

listen to it rain while regret and disdain weep an old fashioned music

and these rearing clouds are beginning to whinny a whole world of auricular towns

you also are raining down marvellous encounters of my life o little drops

it is raining women's voices as if they were dead even in memory

APOLLINAIRE

Alone he rides, alone,
The fair and fatal King:
Dark night is all his own,
That strange and solemn thing.

Which are more full of fate:
The stars; or those sad eyes?
Which are more still and great:
Those brows, or the dark skies?

Although his whole heart yearn
In passionate tragedy,
Never was face so stern
With sweet austerity.

Vanquish'd in life, his death
By beauty made amends:
The passing of his breath
Won his defeated ends.

LIONEL JOHNSON

A Slumber did my Spirit Seal

A slumber did my spirit seal;
    I had no human fears:
She seemed a thing that could not feel
    The touch of earthly years.

No motion has she now, no force;
    She neither hears nor sees;
Rolled round in earth's diurnal course,
    With rocks, and stones, and trees.

WILLIAM WORDSWORTH

That Love is all there is,
Is all we know of Love;
It is enough, the freight should be
Proportioned to the groove.

EMILY DICKINSON

The Robin

When up aloft
I fly and fly,
I see in pools
The shining sky,
And a happy bird
Am I, am I!

When I descend
Towards their brink
I stand, and look,
And stoop, and drink,
And bathe my wings,
And chink and prink.

When winter frost
Makes earth as steel
I search and search
But find no meal,
And most unhappy
Then I feel.

But when it lasts,
And snows still fall,
I get to feel
No grief at all,
For I turn to a cold stiff
Feathery ball!

THOMAS HARDY

ENDPIECE: Photopoems

John Whalley of Wharton School, Salford, has written —
and snapped — this *photopoem*.

Which do you think came first — the picture or the poem?
Perhaps John had the idea for both at the same time.

The Difference

The misty reflection of the city
in the sea
is magical and beautiful.
They flow from side to side
with the gentle breeze.

The sky is dark with rain.
It makes the buildings funny shapes.
The atmosphere changes.

☐ Now you need either to bring in a photograph to write your poem
  round, or to write the poem for which you'll later snap the
  photograph.

Listening to Words

1 Braxo Browns Better

A strange new product, BRAXO, is on the market. What it is we are not sure: perhaps it is a shoe polish, or maybe a gravy. What do you think? The company that produces BRAXO seems interested in one thing: to persuade us BRAXO is best! But then fact is stranger than fiction. Before we believe the company we should look before we leap. Get the idea?

☐ Pair these words off:

green   hue   dawn   hold   day   gold

■ What is the pattern?

☐ If you can guess, then pick from the groups in the poem below the words that best fit the poem:

Nothing Gold Can Stay

Nature's first green is gold,

Her hardest $\left\{\begin{array}{l}\text{colour}\\\text{shade}\\\text{hue}\\\text{tint}\end{array}\right\}$ to hold.

Her early leaf's a flower;
But only so an hour.
Then leaf subsides to leaf.
So Eden sank to grief,

So $\left\{\begin{array}{l}\text{sun-up}\\\text{sunrise}\\\text{morning}\\\text{dawn}\end{array}\right\}$ goes down to day.

Nothing gold can stay.

ROBERT FROST

See the anthology at the end of the chapter for answers.

You have invented a new wonder washing powder called DRAZIL.

You need to think up some catchy slogans to sell it. Here's the first:

DRAZIL DRUBS DIRT

☐ Now invent three or four of your own, and do the same for the new drink FIZZO and the new food BUNZINE.

■ But hold on a minute . . . why are we doing this? And *what* are we doing?

We are *linking words beginning with the same letter:*

> Guinness is good for you
> Double Diamond works wonders
> The Sensational *Sun*

☐ Now make a list of all the slogans you can think of that do this.

☐ Can you add any well-known phrases, like 'Don't drink and drive' and 'fast and furious'?

☐ Go back and look at some of the poems in the book that you have read so far – can you find any more examples?

If we think about the slogans, we can see reasons why the letters are linked.

> – they make the slogan easier to memorise
> – they link ideas

If he can say as you can
Guinness is good for you
How grand to be a Toucan
Just think what Toucan do

■ This is important. Look at *Nothing Gold Can Stay*, by Robert Frost. When is Nature's 'first green' – what time of year? Why does the poet say it is 'gold', not 'blond', 'saffron' or 'yellow'? What special meaning does 'gold' have that the others do not?

The poet is interested in the sound as well as the meaning. The repeated use of the same letter in words that are close together is called *alliteration*. Here is Shakespeare using alliteration with his character Bottom, in *A Midsummer Night's Dream*:

> Whereat, with blade, with bloody blameful blade,
> He bravely broach'd his boiling bloody breast.

and W.S. Gilbert had some fun in *The Mikado*:

> To sit in solemn silence
> In a dull dark dock,
> Awaiting the sensation
> Of a short sharp shock,
> From a cheap and chippy chopper
> On a big black block.

☐ Try yourself: take each of the letters

l m p t w

and find a series of three words that begin with these letters. Try again with four words, and then five.

☐ Write two short poems – the first serious, the second mad. Wildly work on the wily way your wonderful words will bewitch the witless wondrously – wow!

2 Slathery Slithery Hisser

■ What do these words sound like?
buzz   hum   hiss   sizzle   rasp

☐ Can you think of any more? Write them out. Spend some time browsing through a dictionary for more examples. Discuss each one – what does the word sound like? Why?

☐ Read the next poem.

All white and smooth is Flo
A-swimming;
Her lovely dress is plain . . .
No trimming.
A neat delight,
She fans to left and right
The silver-rippled pond.
Behind her, safe and fond,
Her yellow ducklings bob and skim,
Yellow, fluffy, trim.

But all a-waddle and a-spraddle goes Flo
A-walking;
A clacking voice she has
For talking.
In slimy ooze
She plants enormous shoes
And squelches, squat and slow.
Behind her in a row
Her ducklings dip and paddle
And try to spraddle.

GWEN DUNN

Can you find here any more examples of the words we are looking for?

■ What do they do in the poem? Notice the difference between the first and second stanza: what words suit the first stanza? And what words fit the second?

First stanza		**Second stanza**	
smooth	)	a-waddle	)
. . . . .	) sound	. . . .	) sound
neat	)	clacking	)
. . . . . .	) is	. . . .	) is
bob	)	. . . . . .	)
. . . .	) ?	squelches	) ?
. . . .	)	. . . .	)

The words we want *sound* like their meaning. Hear the 'zzzzzzzz' sound in 'buzz', the snake-like 'sssssss' in 'hiss'. This is called *onomatopoeia*.

■ Read through Eleanor Farjeon's *Cat!* and discuss its sounds. What do they suggest about the cat?

Cat!

Cat!
Scat!
Atter her, atter her,
Sleeky flatterer,
Spitfire chatterer,
Scatter her, scatter her
·Off her mat!
Wuff!
Wuff!
Treat her rough!
Git her, git her,
Whiskery spitter!
Catch her, catch her,
Green-eyed scratcher!
Slathery
Slithery
Hisser,
Don't miss her!
Run till you're dithery,
Hithery
Thithery
Pfitts! pfitts!
How she spits!
Spitch! Spatch!
Can't she scratch!
Scritching the bark
Of the sycamore-tree,
She's reached her ark
And's hissing at me
Pfitts! pfitts!
Wuff! wuff!
Scat,
Cat!
That's
That!

ELEANOR FARJEON

Cat sounds	Dog sounds
Whiskery spitter	?
Scritching	?
Pfitts!	?

☐ Choose an animal or creature and write a poem about it, trying to use sounds to suggest the animal's qualities. You can start with words from your list of 'dog sounds'.

3 Mr & Mrs Rhyme

In Book 1 we saw that rhymes of many ('poly-') syllables are often comic. This is because it is difficult to find rhymes for polysyllabic words. We are shocked by the rhyme of 'intellectual' with 'henpecked you all':

But – oh ye lords of ladies intellectual!
Inform us truly, have they not henpecked you all?

LORD BYRON

We laugh because the rhyme is a surprise and because the meanings of the two words are so far apart – but now they are connected by rhyme.

Feminine rhyme occurs when words of two syllables rhyme, and the stress falls on the first syllable of the rhyming word.

■ Read *Piazza Piece*. Pick out the feminine rhymes.

Piazza Piece

– I am a gentleman in a dustcoat trying
To make you hear. Your ears are soft and small
And listen to an old man not at all;
They want the young men's whispering and sighing.
But see the roses on your trellis dying
And hear the spectral singing of the moon –
For I must have my lovely lady soon.
I am a gentleman in a dustcoat trying.

– I am a lady young in beauty waiting
Until my true love comes, and then we kiss.

But what grey man among the vines is this
Whose words are dry and faint as in a dream?
Back from my trellis, sir, before I scream!
I am a lady young in beauty waiting.

JOHN CROWE RANSOM

☐ Now see the effect of rewriting this piece by substituting
monosyllabic rhymes. The first line might be:
– I am a gentleman in a dustcoat who tries

■ What does this do?

Masculine rhyme occurs when words of one syllable rhyme, or when
words of two syllables rhyme but the stress is on the second syllable:

    x /   x /   x /   x /   x /   x /
conceit defeat   concern return   invade replayed

The rhyme is *feminine* when the first syllable is stressed:

    / x   / x   / x
   trying sighing dying

In other words, when the metre is iambic (x /) *in reverse* (/ x). One result of this is to create a 'dying fall' effect:

| stressed syllable – first – heavy sound | ↓ | sound decreasing, |
| unstressed syllable – second – light sound | ↓ | or 'dying'. |

This makes feminine rhyme useful when
  – writing in a reversed iambic metre
  – writing about a subject involving some 'dying fall' idea –
    e.g. the seasons, death, loss
  – writing of these and yet wanting to keep a light, almost
    'breezy' atmosphere

■ If we look at *Piazza Piece* again, we might like to think about the 'gentleman'. Who is he? Why is he in a dustcoat?

■ What have 'roses dying' and 'spectral singing' to do with his presence?

The poem is sombre and chilling: the gentleman is Death himself, coming to destroy youth and beauty. But the atmosphere is still gay, even jokey. Would it be so without the feminine rhymes?

☐ Here is a short poem by Robert Herrick, *On Himself*, with only masculine rhymes. Rewrite the poem, changing some or all of the rhymes to feminine ones. You may need to alter more than just the rhyme word in the line.

On Himself

I will no longer kiss,
I can no longer stay;
The way of all flesh is,
That I must go this day:
Since longer I can't live,
My frolic youths adieu;
My lamp to you I'll give,
And all my troubles too.

ROBERT HERRICK

☐ Here are two possible opening lines for a poem:

      x / x / x / x   /
(a) I saw a man and he was mad

      x / x / x / x / x
(b) I saw a man and he was crazy

Write both poems, using masculine rhymes for (a) and feminine for (b).

■ When you have done this, discuss and compare your two poems.

☐ John Crowe Ransom's *Piazza Piece* alternates masculine and feminine rhymes. Can you combine parts of your poems to include alternating masculine and feminine, or feminine and masculine, rhymes?

ANTHOLOGY 3

From *The Brook*

I chatter over stony ways
In little sharps and trebles,
I bubble into eddying bays,
I babble on the pebbles.

LORD TENNYSON

A Sort of a Song

Let the snake wait under
his weed
and the writing
be of words, slow and quick, sharp
to strike, quiet to wait,
sleepless

– through metaphor to reconcile
the people and the stones.
Compose. (No ideas
but in things) Invent!
Saxifrage is my flower that splits
the rocks.

WILLIAM CARLOS WILLIAMS

Nature's first green is gold,
Her hardest hue to hold.
Her early leaf's a flower;
But only so an hour.
Then leaf subsides to leaf.
So Eden sank to grief,
So dawn goes down to day.
Nothing gold can stay.

ROBERT FROST

An Animal Alphabet

A   The Absolutely Abstemious Ass,
    who resided in a Barrel, and only lived on
    Soda Water and Pickled Cucumbers.

B   The Bountiful Beetle,
    who always carried a Green Umbrella when it didn't rain,
    and left it at home when it did.

C   The Comfortable Confidential Cow,
    who sate in her Red Morocco Armchair and
    toasted her own Bread at the parlour Fire.

D   The Dolomphious Duck,
    who caught spotted frogs for her dinner
    with a Runcible Spoon.

E   The Enthusiastic Elephant,
    who ferried himself across the water with the
    Kitchen Poker and a New pair of Ear-rings.

F   The Fizzgiggious Fish,
    who always walked about upon Stilts,
    because he had no legs.

G   The Good-natured Gray Gull,
    who carried the Old Owl, and his Crimson Carpetbag,
    across the river, because he could not swim.

H   The Hasty Higgeldipiggledy Hen,
who went to market in a Blue Bonnet and Shawl,
and bought a Fish for Supper.

I   The Inventive Indian,
who caught a Remarkable Rabbit in a
Stupendous Silver Spoon.

J   The Judicious Jubilant Jay,
who did up her Back Hair every morning with a Wreath of
    Roses,
Three feathers, and a Gold Pin.

K   The Kicking Kangaroo,
who wore a Pale Pink Muslin dress
with Blue spots.

L   The Lively Learned Lobster,
who mended his own Clothes with
a Needle and Thread.

M   The Melodious Meritorious Mouse.
who played a merry minuet on the
Pianoforte.

N   The Nutritious Newt,
who purchased a Round Plum-pudding,
for his granddaughter.

O   The Obsequious Ornamental Ostrich,
who wore boots to keep his
feet quite dry.

P   The Perpendicular Purple Polly,
who read the Newspaper and ate Parsnip Pie
with his Spectacles.

Q   The Queer Querulous Quail,
who smoked a pipe of tobacco on the top of
a Tin Tea-kettle.

R   The Rural Runcible Raven,
who wore a White Wig and flew away
with the Carpet Broom.

S   The Scroobious Snake,
who always wore a Hat on his Head, for
fear he should bite anybody.

T   The Tumultuous Tom-tommy Tortoise,
who beat a Drum all day long in the
middle of the wilderness.

U   The Umbrageous Umbrella-maker,
whose Face nobody ever saw, because it was
always covered by his Umbrella.

V   The Visibly Vicious Vulture,
who wrote some verses to a Veal-cutlet in a
Volume bound in Vellum.

W   The Worrying Whizzing Wasp,
who stood on a Table, and played sweetly on a
Flute with a Morning Cap.

X   The Excellent Double-extra XX
imbibing King Xerxes, who lived a
long while ago.

Y   The Yonghy-Bonghy-Bo,
whose Head was ever so much bigger than his
Body, and whose Hat was rather small.

Z   The Zigzag Zealous Zebra,
who carried five Monkeys on his back all
the way to Jellibolee.

EDWARD LEAR

Spring and Fall

To a young child

Margaret, are you grieving
Over Goldengrove unleaving?
Leaves, like the things of man, you
With your fresh thoughts care for, can you?
Ah! as the heart grows older
It will come to such sights colder
By and by, nor spare a sigh
Though worlds of wanwood leafmeal lie;
And yet you will weep and know why.
Now no matter, child, the name:
Sorrow's springs are the same.
Nor mouth had, no nor mind, expressed
What heart heard of, ghost guessed:
It is the blight man was born for,
It is Margaret you mourn for.

GERARD MANLEY HOPKINS

My Papa's Waltz

The whiskey on your breath
Could make a small boy dizzy;
But I held on like death:
Such waltzing was not easy.

We romped until the pans
Slid from the kitchen shelf;
My mother's countenance
Could not unfrown itself.

The hand that held my wrist
Was battered on one knuckle;
At every step I missed
My right ear scraped a buckle.

You beat time on my head
With a palm caked hard by dirt,
Then waltzed me off to bed
Still clinging to your shirt.

THEODORE ROETHKE

PART I

On either side the river lie
Long fields of barley and of rye,
That clothe the wold and meet the sky;
And thro' the field the road runs by
     To many-tower'd Camelot;
And up and down the people go,
Gazing where the lilies blow
Round an island there below,
     The island of Shalott.

Willows whiten, aspens quiver,
Little breezes dusk and shiver
Thro' the wave that runs for ever
By the island in the river
     Flowing down to Camelot.
Four gray walls, and four gray towers,
Overlook a space of flowers,
And the silent isle imbowers
     The Lady of Shalott.

By the margin, willow-veil'd,
Slide the heavy barges trail'd
By slow horses; and unhail'd
The shallop flitteth silken-sail'd
     Skimming down to Camelot:
But who hath seen her wave her hand?
Or at the casement seen her stand?
Or is she known in all the land,
     The Lady of Shalott?

Only reapers, reaping early
In among the bearded barley,
Hear a song that echoes cheerly
From the river winding clearly,
     Down to tower'd Camelot:
And by the moon the reaper weary,
Piling sheaves in uplands airy,
Listening, whispers "Tis the fairy
     Lady of Shalott.'

LORD TENNYSON

ENDPIECE: Writing a Play

Death of an Aircraft by Charles Causley tells the story of an aircraft that crash-landed on the island of Crete during the Second World War. This poem makes an excellent play.

> CHARACTERS:
> German officer
> German soldiers
> Villagers
> Three saboteurs
>
> SCENES:
> On the beach
> The village square

☐ Read the poem carefully and make sure you understand the story. Then decide who should have the 'speaking' parts (the words in speech marks). The rest of the poem will be read by narrators – divide the stanzas out between the rest of the group.

☐ The play will be performed in mime. How are you going to suggest setting fire to an aeroplane?

■ Who is the real hero of the story? Who do you think it is?

Death of an Aircraft

One day on our village in the month of July
An aeroplane sank from the sea of the sky,
   White as a whale it smashed on the shore
   Bleeding oil and petrol all over the floor.

The Germans advanced in the vertical heat
To save the dead plane from the people of Crete,
   And round the glass wreck in a circus of snow
   Set seven mechanical sentries to go.

Seven stalking spiders about the sharp sun
Clicking like clockwork and each with a gun
   But at *Come to the Cookhouse* they wheeled about
   And sat down to sausages and sauerkraut.

Down from the mountain burning so brown
Wriggled three heroes from Kastelo town,
   Deep in the sand they silently sank
   And each struck a match for a petrol-tank.

Up went the plane in a feather of fire
As the bubbling boys began to retire
   And, grey in the guardhouse, seven Berliners
   Lost their stripes as well as their dinners.

Down in the village, at murder-stations,
The Germans fell on friends and relations:
   But not a Kastelian snapped an eye
   As he spat in the air and prepared to die.

Not a Kastelian whispered a word
Dressed with the dust to be massacred,
   And squinted up at the sky with a frown
   As three bubbly boys came walking down.

One was sent to the county gaol
Too young for bullets if not for bail,
   But the other two were in prime condition
   To take on a load of ammunition.

In Archonti they stood in the weather
Naked, hungry, chained together:
   Stark as the stones in the market-place,
   Under the eyes of the populace.

Their irons unlocked as their naked hearts
They faced the squad and their funeral-carts.
   The Captain cried, 'Before you're away
   Is there any last word you'd like to say?'

'I want no words,' said one, 'with my lead,
Only some water to cool my head.'
   'Water', the other said, ''s all very fine
   But I'll be taking a glass of wine.

A glass of wine for the afternoon
With permission to sing a signature-tune!'
   And he ran the *raki* down his throat
   And took a deep breath for the leading note.

But before the squad could shoot or say
Like the impala he leapt away
   Over the rifles, under the biers,
   The bullets rattling round his ears.

'Run!' they cried to the boy of stone
Who now stood there in the street alone,
But, 'Rather than bring revenge on your head
It is better for me to die,' he said.

The soldiers turned their machine-guns round
And shot him down with a dreadful sound
Scrubbed his face with perpetual dark
And rubbed it out like a pencil mark.

But his comrade slept in the olive tree
And sailed by night on the gnawing sea,
The soldier's silver shilling earned
And, armed like an archangel, returned.

CHARLES CAUSLEY

Using Words

1 Cauldrons and Saucepans

☐ Find the odd one out!

saucepan cooking-pot cauldron dish microwave

There are reasons why each of these could be chosen as the odd one out; a microwave, for example, is the only one powered by electricity.

■ How many of you picked out *cauldron* as a 'special' word? In what way is it special? What does the word 'cauldron' remind you of?

A cauldron is really just a large iron cooking pot, but it has many supernatural connections! These ideas come into our minds when we think of the word 'cauldron'.

This is an important way in which words work in poetry. All words have meanings of their own, but some words are special: they can remind the reader of many other things as well.

■ Which is the most interesting of these, and why?

thick mist	damp mist
white mist	grey mist
ghostly mist	slight mist

'Ghostly' not only tells us something about the appearance of the mist (white-grey, see-through), but suggests that it is mysterious, creepy, even frightening.

In Shakespeare's play *Macbeth* three witches are busy creating a revolting brew in their cauldron. This is the famous 'Witches Song'. It is great fun to perform this!

Witches' Song

FIRST WITCH Thrice the brinded cat hath mew'd.
SECOND WITCH Thrice and once the hedge-pig whined.
THIRD WITCH Harpier cries: 'Tis time, 'tis time.
FIRST WITCH Round about the cauldron go;
In the poison'd entrails throw.
Toad, that under cold stone

Days and nights hast thirty-one
Swelter'd venom sleeping got,
Boil thou first i' the charmed pot.
ALL Double, double, toil and trouble;
Fire burn and cauldron bubble.
SECOND WITCH Fillet of a fenny snake,
In the cauldron boil and bake;
Eye of newt, and toe of frog,
Wool of bat, and tongue of dog,
Adder's fork, and blind-worm's sting,
Lizard's leg, and howlet's wing,
For a charm of powerful trouble,
Like a hell-broth boil and bubble.
ALL Double, double toil and trouble;
Fire burn and cauldron bubble.
THIRD WITCH Scale of dragon, tooth of wolf,
Witches' mummy, maw and gulf
Of the ravin'd salt-sea shark,
Root of hemlock digg'd i' the dark,
Liver of blaspheming Jew,
Gall of goat, and slips of yew
Sliver'd in the moon's eclipse,
Nose of Turk, and Tartar's lips,
Finger of birth-strangled babe
Ditch-deliver'd by a drab,
Make the gruel thick and slab:
Add thereto a tiger's chaudron,
For the ingredients of our cauldron.
ALL Double, double toil and trouble;
Fire burn and cauldron bubble.
SECOND WITCH Cool it with a baboon's blood,
Then the charm is firm and good.

WILLIAM SHAKESPEARE

☐ Try substituting some of the words in the list at the beginning of this section in place of 'cauldron'. The effect isn't quite the same, is it?

Shakespeare has chosen for the ingredients of the charm things that make the witches' song particularly frightening and gruesome: poisoned entrails, toads, snakes, bats, dog's tongues, livers, and so on. Some of the items suggest danger – the shark and the tiger, for example.

☐ Choose one of these lists of words and include some of them in a poem or paragraph of descriptive writing.

moonlight   creeping   phantom   pale   alone

rage   fire   tiger   gold   smite   revenge

2 Joining Words Together

☐ Match up words from the first column with words from the second.

blind	darkness
green	wind
steel	weapon
total	man
bright	night
howling	leaves
dark	sun

Some of the 'wrong' combinations are more interesting than the right ones!

■ What could be described by the following?

howling darkness
steel wind
blind night

■ Pick other unusual combinations from the list, and discuss how they could be used in a poem or other piece of writing.

Look for unusual word combinations here:

The Three Winds

The hard blue winds of March
shake the young sheep
and flake the long stone walls;
now from the gusty grass
comes the horned music of rams,
and plovers fall out of the sky
filling their wings with snow.

Tired of this northern tune
the winds turn soft
blowing white butterflies
out of the dog-rose hedges,
and schoolroom songs are full
of boys' green cuckoos
piping the summer round

Till August sends at last
its brick-red breath
over the baking wheat and blistered poppy,

brushing with feathered hands
the skies of brass,
with dreams of river moss
my thirst's delirium.

LAURIE LEE

■ What do you think is meant by these phrases?

> hard blue winds
> gusty grass
> boys' green cuckoos
> brick-red breath
> skies of brass

☐ Look at the list of words on page 48. Choose one unusual pair and include it in a poem, or find other interesting combinations of your own.

3 Swift Movers

■ Swifts are very fast-moving birds. Discuss this list of verbs, and say which ones you think are sensible, and what they mean.

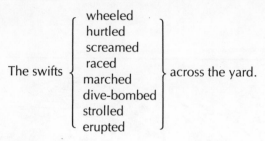

The swifts
- wheeled
- hurtled
- screamed
- raced
- marched
- dive-bombed
- strolled
- erupted

across the yard.

This section is about those useful words, *verbs*.

☐ Find the verb in this sentence.

The swifts were flying across the fields.

Can you improve it by finding *one* word to replace 'were flying' that gives a suggestion of speed?

■ Pick out the most effective sentence from this pair:

The snake was crawling across the road.
The snake was slithering across the road.

'Crawled' can't be right, can it? Snakes don't really crawl. 'Slithered' is a better verb to describe the movement of a snake, but you may be able to think of a more unusual verb. Make up a sentence using it. Decide: what sort of snake is it? Is it big and slow, or small and fast? Does it sneak up on you, or leap out at your from a tree and slither down the back of your neck?

There is another change we can make. It is nearly always better to get rid of 'were' and 'was':

The snake slithered across the road.

☐ If you have used 'was' in your snake sentence, get rid of it!

☐ Now write a list of verbs to describe the movement of a spider down the back of your neck!

Read this poem by Ted Hughes, paying particular attention to the underlined verbs.

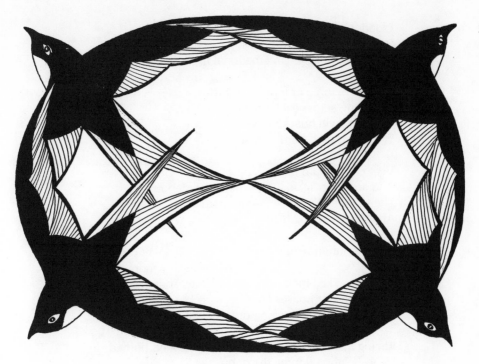

Swifts

Fifteenth of May. Cherry blossom. The swifts
Materialise at the tip of a long scream
Of needle. 'Look! They're back! Look!' And they're gone
On a steep

Controlled scream of skid
Round the house-end and away under the cherries. Gone.
Suddenly flickering in sky summit, three or four together,
Gnat-whisp frail, and hover-searching, and listening

For air-chills – are they too early? With a bowing
Power-thrust to left, then to right, then a flicker they
Tilt into a slide, a tremble for balance,
Then a lashing down disappearance

Behind elms.
             They've made it again,
Which means the globe's still working, the Creation's
Still waking refreshed, our summer's
Still all to come –
             And here they are, here they are again

Erupting across yard stones
Shrapnel-scatter terror. Frog-gapers,
Speedway goggles, international mobsters —

A bolas of three or four wire screams
Jockeying across each other
On their switchback wheel of death.
They swat past, hard-fletched,

Veer on the hard air, toss up over the roof,
And are gone again. Their mole-dark labouring,
Their lunatic limber scramming frenzy
And their whirling blades

Sparkle out into blue —
                              Not ours any more.
Rats ransacked their nests so now they shun us.
Round luckier houses now
They crowd their evening dirt-track meetings,

Racing their discords, screaming as if speed-burned,
Head-height, clipping the doorway
With their leaden velocity and their butterfly lightness,
Their too much power, their arrow-thwack into the eaves.

Every year a first-fling, nearly-flying
Misfit flopped in our yard,
Groggily somersaulting to get airborne.
He bat-crawled on his tiny useless feet, tangling his flails

Like a broken toy, and shrieking thinly
Till I tossed him up — then suddenly he flowed away under
His bowed shoulders of enormous swimming power,
Slid away along levels wobbling

On the fine wire they have reduced life to,
And crashed among the raspberries.
Then followed fiery hospital hours
In a kitchen. The moustached goblin savage

Nested in a scarf. The bright blank
Blind, like an angel, to my meat-crumbs and flies.
Then eyelids resting. Wasted clingers curled.
The inevitable balsa death.
                              Finally burial

For the husk
Of my little Apollo —

The charred scream
Folded in its huge power.

TED HUGHES

■ Discuss the underlined verbs and try to decide why Ted Hughes
chose them. If you are not sure about the meaning of some of the
words in this poem, you should check in a dictionary.

☐ Write a poem describing movement. The moving thing described
need not be living. Concentrate on finding really effective verbs to
describe the various movements.

4 Which Word?

In this chapter we have discussed how
- words can be used to remind us of other things 'cauldron' =
'witches')
- words can be used in unusual combinations ('blue wind')
- verbs are important in making writing effective ('They swat
past')

This poem shows all of these lessons in action.

Pigeons

They paddle with staccato feet
In powder-pools of sunlight,
Small blue busybodies
Strutting like fat gentlemen
With hands clasped
Under their swallowtail coats;
And, as they stump about,
Their heads like tiny hammers
Tap at imaginary nails
In non-existent walls.
Elusive ghosts of sunshine
Slither down the green gloss
Of their necks an instant, and are gone.

54

Summer hangs drugged from sky to earth
In limpid fathoms of silence:
Only warm dark dimples of sound
Slide like slow bubbles
From the contented throats.

Raise a casual hand —
With one quick gust
They fountain into the air.

RICHARD KELL

■ What does 'busybodies' suggest that 'busy bodies' does not?
■ What does 'strutting' suggest that 'walking' does not?
■ What does 'fountain' suggest that 'fly away' does not?

■ Here are some unusual word combinations. Why does Richard
Kell put these words together?

    staccato feet
    powder-pools
    ghosts of sunshine
    Summer hangs drugged
    fathoms of silence
    warm dark dimples

■ Here is the first section of *Pigeons*, rewritten with different verbs.
Why are the original verbs better?

> They plod with staccato feet
> In powder-pools of sunlight,
> Small blue busybodies
> Strolling like fat gentlemen
> With hands clasped
> Under their swallowtail coats;
> And, as they march about,
> Their heads like tiny hammers
> Knock at imaginary nails
> In non-existent walls.
> Elusive ghosts of sunshine
> Move down the green gloss
> Of their necks an instant, and are gone.

An unusual verb in the poem is 'to fountain', and you have already
discussed the special meaning it has that 'fly away' does not. Here
are some more unusual verbs. Not all of them are in regular use!
Discuss meanings for them.

to dog	to ghost
to thumb	to green
to caterpillar	to boy *or* to girl
to steel	to brilliant

☐ Here are some *nouns, verbs* and *adjectives*. Roll a dice to pick one
from each column, then combine them in the first line of a poem.
You can change them a little if you wish: 'flight' could become the
verb 'fly', and 'fade' could become the adjective 'faded', for
example. If you rolled '1, 1, 1' your first line might be:
   Thin dragonflies in flight skimmed the pond
The words all come from the poems in the anthology at the end of
this chapter.

nouns	verbs	adjectives
1 flight	1 skim	1 thin
2 pleasure	2 limp	2 wild
3 stable	3 flit	3 frosted
4 steel	4 dash	4 stray
5 mountains	5 stab	5 screaming
6 curves	6 fade	6 noisy

☐ When you have exhausted these, pick another six nouns, verbs
and adjectives from the poems in the anthology and start again.

ANTHOLOGY 4

The Flight of Birds

The crow goes flopping on from wood to wood,
The wild duck wherries to the distant flood,
The starnels hurry o'er in merry crowds,
And overhead whew by like hasty clouds;
The wild duck from the meadow-water plies
And dashes up the water as he flies;
The pigeon suthers by on rapid wing,
The lark mounts upward at the call of spring.
In easy flights above the hurricane
With doubled neck high sails the noisy crane.
Whizz goes the pewit o'er the ploughman's team,
With many a whew and whirl and sudden scream;
And lightly fluttering to the tree just by,
In chattering journeys whirls the noisy pie;
From bush to bush slow swees the screaming jay,
With one harsh note of pleasure all the day.

JOHN CLARE

There came a wind like a bugle;
It quivered through the grass,
And a green chill upon the heat
So ominous did pass
We barred the windows and the doors
As from an emerald ghost;
The doom's electric moccasin
That very instant passed.
On a strange mob of panting trees,
And fences fled away,
And rivers where the houses ran
Those looked that lived – that day.
The bell within the steeple wild
The flying tidings told.
How much can come
And much can go,
And yet abide the world!

EMILY DICKINSON

First, boys out of school went out of their way home
To detonate the windows; at each smash
Piping with delight and skipping for fright
Of a ghost of the old man popping over his hedge,
Shrieking and nodding from the gate.
Then the silence palled, since it was only breaking the silence.
The rain sluiced through the starred gaps,
Crept up walls into brick; frost bit and munched;
Weeds craned in and leant on the doors.
Now it is a plot without trees let into the wood
Piled high with tangle and tousle
Buried parapets and roots picking at the last mortar
Though the chimney still stands sheathed in leaves
And you can see for the time being where in a nook
A briony burst its pot with a shower of roots
And back through the press of shrubs and stems
Deep-coils into the woods.

PETER REDGROVE

Pied Beauty

Glory be to God for dappled things —
   For skies of couple-colour as a brinded cow;
     For rose-moles all in stipple upon trout that swim;
Fresh-firecoal chestnut-falls; finches' wings;
   Landscape plotted and pieced — fold, fallow and plough;
     And all trades, their gear and tackle and trim.

All things counter, original, spare, strange;
   Whatever is fickle, freckled (who knows how?)
     With swift, slow; sweet, sour; adazzle, dim;
He fathers-forth whose beauty is past change:
        Praise him.

GERARD MANLEY HOPKINS

ENDPIECE: Broadsheets

In the nineteenth century, poems were often printed on single sheets and sold in the streets; there is a picture of one here. The poems were often thrilling and not-too-accurate accounts of current events such as the Battle of Trafalgar.

☐ You can produce your own broadsheets. You will need to write or type your 'current events' poem onto a sheet of paper, and illustrate the sheets with appropriate drawings. If possible, these could be photocopied and sold for a small sum, perhaps to raise funds for a good cause. If you cannot do this, your broadsheets would make an attractive wall display.

New Ways of Looking

1 Similes and Metaphors

In the first book we discussed *similes* and *metaphors*. To remind you, here are the definitions again.

Simile. A comparison using 'as' or 'like'

> Love is like a red, red Rose
> The corn is as high as an elephant's eye
> Your teeth are like stars . . . they come out at night.

Metaphor. A comparison that suggests that the thing described is something quite different.

> The sea-gulls dive-bombed the dog . . . (This suggests the gulls are aircraft.)
> 'You dirty rat!'

Metaphors and similes are part of the poet's *imagery*. Imagery includes all pictures, sounds and feelings used by the poet to make the meaning of the poem clear.

Now read these two passages. They are both about millipedes.

THE WOODLAND SNAKE MILLIPEDE (*Cylindroiulus sylvarum*) is found in leaf litter on the floors of both deciduous and coniferous woodlands. The number of limbs is variable, but generally numbers about 100. Millipedes live on decaying vegetation, but can be a pest on soft fruit, particularly strawberries.

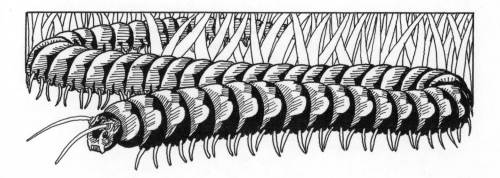

Millipede

A column's on the move. Like this
Napoleon's *Grande Armée*
Set out for Moscow – close order,
Slightly out of step. A single organism
But noisy, with colours.

The legs gooseberry prickles
Which press forward, as the fibres
Of a toothbrush, riffled, spring upright
Again. The spines though
Are bayonets, and have the look

Of embattled porcupine in a forest
Of speargrass. (Who was it
Called states a sack of these?) An ordered
Anarchy then, in the guise
Of a fragment of coconut matting.

ROY BENNETT

■ Which gives you more information about the subject? Which helps
   you picture the millipede, and imagine how it moves?

■ Do either of them tell us anything about the author's *feelings* about
   the subject?

Here is an encyclopaedia entry on rats.

   Rats are rodents, or gnawing animals, that are found in all parts of
   the world. In Britain there are two species, the black rat, and the
   far more common brown rat.
      Rats are serious pests as they damage foodstuffs and can cause
   structural damage and even fires by gnawing through cables. They
   often enter buildings by travelling through sewers . . .

□ Using some of this information, write a poem making it clear what
   you feel about them. Use imagery to express what you feel. If you
   can't stand the thought of writing about rats, choose a different
   subject and use an encyclopaedia to start you off.

2 Next Day

In Book 1 we read a poem called *A New Year* by Wes Magee, that
described a violent snowstorm on New Year's Eve. This poem
continues the story.

Sheep, Buried

Overnight, an airborne invasion.
Blizzard's shock troops have taken the low hills
    And this morning's monochrome standard
Unfurls stiffly across a raw landscape.
    Colour has been confined to barracks.
A steel wind keens the no man's land between
    Snowfield and sky: a shivering of distance.

Rag-clad, like Siberian lifers,
We stump uphill to where the field's hedge
    Has vanished beneath a crested drift.
Here lie sheep, buried. Instinct led them to
    Expect shelter from the savage storm,
Like punters we must thrust six-foot canes down
    Through snow to prod the earth's frozen muscle.

We string out, figures on a bleak ridge.
Shove, bend, haul and straighten. Repeat. Repeat.
    The ewe's body, when struck, feels tough
As a tractor tyre. Our shouts echo long
    Before shovels arrive and we dig,
Fox-holing in a winter's warfare, and
    There she is, wool ice-starred, her nose snow-slushed.

We manhandle her clear, our curses
Kindling the air. A kick and she staggers
    Towards a scarp of field where snow lies thin.
Now we lean on shovels, the silence sharp,
    A panorama brittle with frost.
The sun emerges, pallid survivor,
    A prisoner led out for exercise.

WES MAGEE

Wes Magee writes:

A New Year and *Sheep, Buried* were both written about events on New Year's Eve and New Year's Day at Totleigh Barton Manor House, which is in an isolated part of Devon. The day after the blizzard struck I joined others as we helped a local farmer to rescue buried sheep. The poem is very much an observer's report on the front-line state of play. I worked hard on the poem, with many, many drafts, to fully realise the scene and to convey the feel of cold, desolation, silence-quality, and the actual facts of digging out sheep. It is worth noting that another 'digger' (George MacBeth) has written and published a poem on that exact theme and experience . . . *A Poem for Breathing*. George's descriptions often isolate different moments and follow new tracks of thought. This is perhaps one of the few instances where two writers, working apart and alone, worried away at a shared experience.

In fact, the rescue was successful and we found many sheep.

You will find *A Poem for Breathing* on page 84.

Totleigh Barton

Some metaphors:

    A steel wind
    Blizzard's shock troops
    Curses kindling the air

Some similes:

    Rag-clad, like Siberian lifers (Prisoners in a Russian labour camp)
    Like punters we must thrust six-foot canes (What is a punt?)
    The ewe's body . . . feels tough as a tractor tyre.

■ Find these similes and metaphors in the poem. How do they help in telling us what the experience was like for the 'diggers', and how the poet felt about the experience?

One way of looking at metaphors is to find out what the comparison is with. For example in 'A steel wind' the comparison is with a steel door, or perhaps a steel weapon.

■ What are the comparisons with here? Fill in these gaps:

1 .... shock troops
2 .... kindling the air
3 .... has been confined to barracks

☐ The sense of *touch* is important in this poem. Try to imagine the feel of that 'steel wind' or the feel of the sheep's body as it is prodded by the pole. Try to make up *images* (metaphors and similes) to describe the following:

> Walking in wet clothes after rain
> Touching a fish under water
> Holding a small animal
> Lying on a hot, sandy beach

☐ Use one of these ideas, or 'touch' images of your own, to form the basis of a poem or piece of descriptive writing.

Wes Magee writes about how two writers can share an experience, and yet write about it very differently. You can try this if your class have shared an experience, such as a school visit, or a sporting fixture. Write about it without discussing it first, then compare the different points of view in your writing.

3 Sharing Experiences

In the last section we saw that imagery isn't just an addition to a poem, like adding icing to a cake to make it look better.

Imagery helps us to understand:
> – What the poem is about.
> – What the poet is trying to say about the subject of the poem.

Imagery is a way in which the poet *shares* an experience with us.

Mastering the Craft

To make the big time you must learn
The basic moves: left jab and hook,
The fast one-two, right-cross; the block
And counter-punch; the way to turn

Opponents on the ropes; the feint
To head or body; uppercut;
To move inside the swing and set
Your man up for the kill. But don't
Think that this is all; a mere
Beginning only. It is through
Fighting often you will grow
Accomplished in manoeuvres more
Subtle than the text-books know:
How to change your style to meet
The unexpected move that might
Leave you open to the blow
That puts the lights out for the night.

The same with poets: they must train,
Practise metre's footwork, learn
The old iambic left and right,
To change the pace and how to hold
The big punch till the proper time,
Jab away with accurate rhyme;
Adapt the style or be knocked cold.
But first the groundwork must be done.
Those poets who have never learnt
The first moves of the game, they can't
Hope to win.
            Yet here comes one,
No style at all, untrained and fat,
Who still contrives to knock you flat.

VERNON SCANNELL

Vernon Scannell says that writing a poem is like boxing! This doesn't
seem very likely. This table may help make it clear what he is talking
about:

	boxing	writing
Learn the rules	√	√
Have a sense of rhythm	√	√
Be flexible to cope with unexpected situations	√	√
Learn to vary your pace	√	√
Hold back your best until the right moment	√	√

■ Discuss how these things work for boxing and writing poems.
When writing poems, who is the 'opponent'? What do you think is
meant by 'metre's footwork' and 'The old iambic left and right'?
(See Chapter 2, on rhythm.)

In boxing, if you do not learn the skills, you are going to be in a difficult situation! You will end up knocked out on the floor. Vernon Scannell uses this comparison to tell us that unless you succeed in 'mastering the craft', something similar (though not so painful!) will happen to you when you try to write a poem.

You may not be surprised to learn that Vernon Scannell was a boxer!

■ Does the comparison with boxing
   – help to explain what the poem is about?
   – tell us how the author feels about the subject?

The last section of the poem seems to contradict what has been said before, someone totally untrained and unskilled has somehow managed to deliver a knock-out punch.

■ Could the same work for writing poems?

This poem compares people and trees.

With People, So With Trees

With people, so with trees: where there are groups
Of either, men or trees, some will remain
Aloof while others cluster where one stoops
To breathe some dusky secret. Some complain

And some gesticulate and some are blind;
Some toss their heads above green towns; some freeze
For lack of love in copses of mankind;
Some laugh; some mourn; with people, so with trees.

MERVYN PEAKE

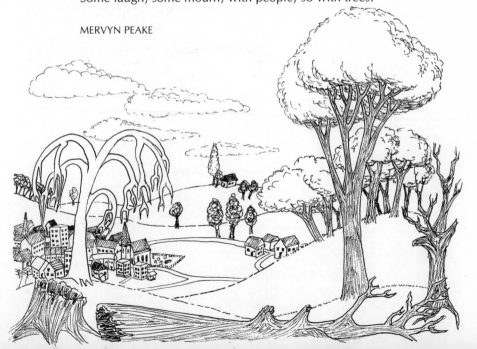

□ Write a list of sentences that apply to people and trees as they appear in this poem.

4 Things as People

Winter the Huntsman

Through his iron glades
Rides Winter the Huntsman.
All colour fades
As his horn is heard sighing.

Far through the forest
His wild hooves crash and thunder
Till many a branch
Is torn asunder.

And the red reynard creeps
To his hole near the river,
The copper leaves fall
And the bare trees shiver

As night creeps from the ground,
Hides each tree from its brother,
And each dying sound
Reveals yet another.

Is it Winter the Huntsman
Who gallops through his iron glades,
Cracking his cruel whip
To the gathering shades?

OSBERT SITWELL

In *With People, So With Trees* by Mervyn Peake, trees were
compared with people. *Winter the Huntsman* does this, too. Winter
is a cruel huntsman bringing death to the forest, rather like Wes
Magee's 'Blizzard's shock troops' in *Sheep, Buried*.

■ We often talk about ships and cars as if they were people. Why do
   you think we do this? Why are they usually described as female?

Here is a list of 'things', and a list of 'qualities'. Try matching them
up. Some of the 'qualities' will fit more than one 'thing'.

things	qualities
summer	angry
a river	cheerful
fear	evil
autumn	rich
the wind	old
time	youthful
spring	lazy
a mountain	stern
	vicious

Describing non-human things as if they were people is called
personification. This is a way in which writers give 'things' a
character of their own.

The *Canterbury Tales* were written by Geoffrey Chaucer around
1380. Language was very different then, and the version of part of the
'Pardoner's Tale' below has been modernised. A boy is telling his
masters how a friend of his met his fate:

From *Canterbury Tales*

Suddenly, he was killed last night,
When drunk; for, sitting on a bench upright
There came a secret thief, men call him death,
That in this country all men slayeth.
And with his spear he cut his heart in two,
And went on his way without any more ado.

GEOFFREY CHAUCER

Personification is a very useful way in which poets can express their
feelings about non-human things. This time it is Death that is
personified; he has become a 'secret thief'.

■ If Death is a thief, what does he steal? What does Chaucer want to tell us about Death?

☐ Earlier in this section, you sorted out 'things' and 'qualities'. Use one of these ideas in a poem of your own.

☐ Write a story about a ship or car as if it were a person.

ANTHOLOGY 5

Winter Warfare

Colonel Cold strode up the line
   (Tabs of rime and spurs of ice),
Stiffened all where he did glare,
   Horses, men, and lice.

Visited a forward post,
   Left them burning, ear to foot;
Fingers stuck to biting steel,
   Toes to frozen boot.

Stalked on into No Man's Land,
   Turned the wire to fleecy wool,
Iron stakes to sugar sticks
   Snapping at a pull.

Those who watched with hoary eyes
   Saw two figures gleaming there;
Hauptman Kalte, Colonel Cold,
   Gaunt, in the grey air.

Stiffly tinkling spurs they moved
   Glassy eyed, with glinting heel
Stabbing those who lingered there
   Torn by screaming steel.

EDGELL RICKWORD

From *On the Death of a Fair Infant, Dying of a Cough*

O Fairest flower! no sooner blown but blasted,
Soft silken primrose fading timelessly,

Summer's chief honour, if thou hads't out-lasted
Bleak Winter's force that made thy blossom dry;
For he being amorous on that lovely dye
That did thy cheek envermeil, thought to kiss,
But killed, alas, and then bewailed his fatal bliss.

JOHN MILTON

[amorous = lovestruck; dye = day; envermeil = turn red.]

I like to see it lap the miles,
And lick the valleys up,
And stop to feed itself at tanks
And then prodigious step

Around a pile of mountains,
And supercilious peer
In shanties by the sides of roads,
And then a quarry pare

To fit its sides
And crawl between
Complaining all the while
In horrid, hooting stanza,
Then chase itself down hill
And neigh like Boanerges,
Then prompter than a star,
Stop, docile and omnipotent,
At its own stable door.

EMILY DICKINSON

The Skaters

Black swallows swooping or gliding
In a flurry of entangled loops and curves;
The skaters skim over the frozen river.
And the grinding click of their skates as they impinge upon the
    surface,
Is like the brushing together of thin wing-tips of silver.

J.G. FLETCHER

ENDPIECE: Riddles

Thirty white horses on a red hill
First they champ
Then they stamp
Then they stand still

You will remember this riddle if you have read *The Hobbit*, by
J.R.R. Tolkien. The answer is 'teeth'.
 Here is another old favourite:

In marble halls as white as milk,
Lined with a skin as soft as silk,
Within a fountain crystal-clear,
A golden apple doth appear.
No doors there are to this stronghold,
Yet thieves break in and steal the gold.

The answer to this is at the bottom of this page.

Not all riddles are short poems; one of the best known is the riddle of
the sphinx. Find out what this is, and the story behind it. However,
traditional English riddles often are short poems based on a
metaphor. Here is one translated from Anglo-Saxon:

When it is the earth I tread, make tracks upon the water
or keep the houses, hushed is my clothing,
clothing that can hoist me above the house ridges
at times toss me into the tall heaven
where the strong cloud-wind carries me on
over cities and countries; accoutrements that
throb out sound, thrilling strokes
deep-soughing song, as I sail alone
over field and flood, faring on,
resting nowhere. My name is —.

Translated by MICHAEL ALEXANDER

☐ Have a class riddle competition. Write as many riddles as you
 like, but keep the answers to yourself! Make a display of the
 riddles and invite the class to work out the answers.

Answers to riddles (above)
'In marble halls . . .': An egg.
'When it is the earth I tread . . .': Mute swan.

Finding a Subject

1 Starting Points

Sometimes, finding an idea to write about is the most difficult part of writing poetry. Poets often use exercises such as the ones you have tried in this series. The object of doing them, though, is to help improve by practice the way they write. To produce really good poems, poets need to explore subjects that are important to them.

In Book 1 we suggested a number of ways in which the first idea for a poem comes. There are many other ways and you may be able to think of some yourself.

> A visit to a particular place
> Relationships with other people
> Unexpected incidents
> Experiences that have been important to the writer
> Reading books, seeing films, listening to music, looking at
>   pictures
> Treasured objects
> Powerful personal feelings and problems
> Memories

We are going to look at five examples of writers using these starting points. As usual, we shall suggest responses to these poems, but there will be opportunity for you to develop your own writing from there.

2 People

There are very many ways to write about people. You could write, for example, about:

> Members of your family
> Other people you know well
> People you have never met, but have heard about
> People from the past that you remember
> Somebody you see only briefly

On days when the cancer was worse and Dad
Sat limp as a damp flannel, he would need
His greying face shaved. 'I'm not so bad
Today,' he claimed as I sat shrinking from the deed.
The razor scuffed across his cheek; no good.
He was difficult to approach; the angle was wrong.
Some more soft soap might do the trick. 'Would
You stop?' he said. 'That's fine, that's fine son.'
He wasn't shaved at all but Mother rinsed
His face while I feigned a reason to leave.
'I'll be better tomorrow,' he said. I convinced
Myself he would be: we all wanted a reprieve.
Two years of pain finished in a hospital bed
With the last lie. 'He went peacefully,' a nurse said.

JIM C. WILSON

Jim C. Wilson writes:

The first line just came to me one day in the street (about three years
after my father's death). I built the poem from the one line which I
thought had a disturbing casualness about it – as if the weather were
being described.

■ The poem is called *The Last Lie*. How many lies can you find in
the poem? Why were people telling these lies?

This 'time chart' shows how this poem developed:

> The experiences
>
> ↓
>
> Three years later, a line comes into the author's head
>
> ↓
>
> The writer starts to build up the poem
>
> ↓
>
> The poem is completed

Frances Cornford saw a woman from a train, and wrote this about the experience:

To a Lady seen from a Train

O why do you walk through the fields in gloves,
    Missing so much and so much?
O fat white woman whom nobody loves,
Why do you walk through the fields in gloves,
When the grass is soft as the breast of doves
    And shivering-sweet to the touch?
O why do you walk through the fields in gloves,
    Missing so much and so much?

FRANCES CORNFORD

■ What is this woman missing? Why do you think that seeing this
woman made such an impression on the poet? Why are the gloves
particularly mentioned?

☐ Write a short description of a real person, and of an imaginary
one. (Make sure the other members of the class do not know the
'real' person.) Read out the descriptions and let the rest of the class
guess which one is real.

☐ Choose one of the suggested ways of writing about people for a
piece of writing of your own.

3 Reading and Looking

Many poets have written poems after experiencing works by others –
music, books, film and paintings, for example, or even watching
television programmes.

The War Game

Watching rugger, you see the bodies piling up.
When the whistle blows, they peel off – one by one –
Like wasps disturbed at an apple.
The last ones most slowly, with a crushed weariness.
Occasionally one is left – a leg injured, a head.
Sometimes, with help, he limps off. He can be replaced.

We are now talking about a game where they don't get up.
No blowing of whistles would make them walk away.
There are no rules. When they're down, they're down.
And the wonderful thing about this game is: everybody can play it.
Men, women, children. A game that's popular – in every sense!

GAVIN EWART

Gavin Ewart writes:

This poem was the direct result of watching rugger matches on the
telly. When a maul or scrum collapses or players pile into a tackle
they do indeed look like wasps coming one by one out of a rotten
apple (the stripes often worn by players make this image more real)
when the whistle is blown. The ones at the bottom of the heap,
however much you expect them to be harmed by the pressure,
slowly disengage themselves and turn out not to have been hurt at
all, though occasionally a player is injured.

For this poem, here is another chart:

Watching the match
↓
Thinking about the injured players
↓
Thinking about the much more serious 'game' of nuclear war
↓
Writing the poem

A nuclear war, the poem says, wouldn't be like this. People knocked over by nuclear blast and waves of fire don't get up again. Everybody will be involved, it will be truly democratic – except perhaps for Governments and Royal Persons in deep shelters – a game that anybody can play. In fact, a game that everybody may be forced to play.

Notice how Gavin Ewart has moved from a small matter (the match) to a very important one (nuclear warfare). The match itself was only the start of the process of making a poem.

☐ These pictures may provide the starting point for a poem. Alternatively, cut out a picture from a magazine and use it to start a poem off. You could mount a picture and poem display.

4 Using Memories

Poets write because they have something important to say, but vivid
and important experiences don't come along to order! When you are
asked to write a poem in class, for example, you may find it difficult
to come up with an interesting experience to write about.

This is where our memory can help out. Jim Wilson's poem was
written three years after the events described in it, and some poets
have written about incidents in their lives that took place many years
before.

Matt Simpson writes about using memories in his poetry:

I have a bad memory. If I don't keep my diary close to hand I have
problems keeping promises and fulfilling duties. I'm hopeless at dates
and fitting faces to names. Birthdays, anniversaries land me in
trouble; I've long been given up on by godchildren. I even once
wrote on the fly-leaf of a book I gave to my daughter 'for Catherine
on her 19th birthday' when she was actually 18 and then dated it
with the date of my son's birthday!

Of course, I'm not always as bad as that. But the point I want to
make is that there is a connection between my (either blank or
dithering) memory and my poems. When a memory does surface in
me, it needs to be grabbed hold of, pinned down, interrogated. (Why
have I suddenly thought of this? What's the significance of this
intrusive memory? What's it trying to tell me?) Writing a poem is a bit
like setting out on an archaeological expedition. (Is there gold? Will
the tomb be empty?)

What causes memories to surface? Sometimes they just seem to
come spontaneously – usually into a kind of broodiness on my part;
sometimes they are evoked by an overheard remark or by the sudden
awareness that something is 'out of place'; sometimes they spill over
from other poems that I have written; occasionally they are
stimulated by things I have read. And nearly always they are located
in specific places. Though I want to know about the human meanings
inscribed in a place, I invariably, when I read my own poems to
myself, 'see' a place – a room, a street, a stretch of shore I used to
walk along when I was a lad . . . The memory, the mood, the 'place',
the feeling of something out-of-place synchronise with or are fused
with (if there's the hope of a poem) a phrase, a sentence, a line. It's
as if, to use a metaphor from fishing, the float has bobbed and you
know you've had a bite. Now the concentration has to be in earnest,
the hard writing has to begin.

The following poem brings to the surface some of the things I have
been describing. It appeared in a collection in which nearly all the
poems explored my early life, growing up in Bootle on Merseyside.
Quite by chance one day I discovered that I was in a Bootle street I

knew by name but had not actually set foot in before this occasion.
But my father had once grown up in this street and it was here that
several things which were of real significance to me had their origin.

Blossom Street

Memories and places. A jumbled itinerary
of journeying undergone.
                                        It is myself
I am compiling, rearranging a town
for reasons I don't understand.

Yesterday I parked, pulled in across
a residue of snow and walked
around the corner to a shop I'd found
last year – student cast-offs, books
in clumsy piles.
                            What is it that
accuses? I walked the length
of Blossom Street,
                                    caught by a name
from thirty years ago, a terraced street,
ancestral place I'd never seen before.

But from here my father as a boy
was off-loaded to a Training Ship.
This is where the gibings start.
From here his ruined boyhood comes
spilling into what I have become.
This is where the sea begins its mutterings.

The place a memory, the memory a place.

MATT SIMPSON

5 Poems and Places

People like places! This may be because:

> The places are particularly beautiful or historic
> The people have lived there a long time
> Something very important to them happened there

This is a picture of the Bargate, a mediaeval archway in Southampton, England. Brian Hinton's poem is about this building, and the poem shares its shape.

Bargate

Stately and imperfect, bisecting a maze of traffic
its lock-ups wait in vain, shuttered as this forgotten
centre, tram-scarred. Steps lead up steeply, begotten
by the centuries on stone, falling away like rough magic.

Magic	in	dredging	Unloaded
is	this	distant	here
guarded	storehouse	sea	to
by	of	ways	feed
time	a	to	the
eroded	working	disinter	nation's
Ascupart	shore	treasure	heart

Hearts crack, my distant ancestors
toiling on the docks and railways,
bringing up black slate dust
the great ship of Southampton

breaking bones and spirit, in
hitching for work as far as Wales
with each breath. Under full sail
tight rigged with dead men's limbs.

Limbs trembling, I climb to
from my great height of folly
shores decked with shipyards
a savage and slumbering giant

this crow's nest to reinstate
the working body spread beneath
cranes bowing to an unseen breeze;
laid on the earth as if in state.

Brian Hinton writes:

Bargate was really written as a cure for homesickness, which might seem a bit odd, as it is about a mediaeval building!

Let me explain. Most people nowadays have to leave their home town – to go to college, to get a job – and I am no exception. I was born and brought up in Southampton, so I chose to write about its most famous landmark, the Bargate.

Indian tribes erect a totem pole, with carvings of the animals or plants they hold sacred. I have tried to do the same with words, not only writing about this place but actually making the words form the shape of the building, with gaps for the central arch and three arrow slits. You can do the same. Why not try to write poems in the shape of a football stand, or a bird, or a friend, or anything . . . .

This poem is about my sense of heritage, my ancestors all growing up in the same place – though granddad had to literally walk to South Wales to find work in the 1930s, getting a job in the slate mines. It is very important to me, this sense of place, and I see the town that I grew up in as a sleeping giant, waiting to come to mastery.

English writers have always been attracted to a sense of place – think of Thomas Hardy and the novels he set in Wessex, or Emily Brontë's portrait of the Yorkshire Moors in *Wuthering Heights*, or Charles Dickens' marvellous descriptions of Victorian London. These writers have all responded to the mood of the place they describe as much as its physical appearance, and in all three examples the characters of the novels seem to grow out of the landscape that helped produce them.

We are all moulded by the place where we grew up; for better or worse we always see the world partly through our memories of childhood. Funnily enough, the more specific the setting of a poem or a play or a novel, the more universal it is. After all, however restless we are, none of us can live in more than one place at a time!

☐ There are a number of ways in which you could tackle writing about places. These questions may help with ideas.

> Town or country?
> Real or imaginary?
> A place you know well, or somewhere you see for the first time?
> How do you *feel* about the place? (Are you homesick? Angry about a place spoiled by pollution or ugly development? Bored? Excited? Frightened?)

☐ There is a well-known poem beginning with these lines:

I remember, I remember,
The house where I was born . . .

Start a poem of your own with these lines. Before you do, read
again what Matt Simpson says about memories.

6 Treasured Objects

Objects can often produce ideas for interesting poetry. In this section
George MacBeth describes how he came to write the poem *The
Drawer*. He describes himself as a 'tactile' poet; that is, one for whom
the sense of touch is very important. Holding an object tells us about
its weight and texture; it can also bring back memories of past events
in the same way that places and names do for Matt Simpson and
Brian Hinton.

The Drawer

Their belongings were buried side by side
In a shallow bureau drawer. There was her
Crocodile handbag, letters, a brooch,
All that was in the bedside cupboard
And a small green jar she'd had for flowers.

My father's were in an envelope:
A khaki lanyard, crushed handkerchief,
Twelve cigarettes, a copying-pencil,
All he had on him when he was killed
Or all my mother wanted to keep.

I put them together, seven years ago.
Now that we've moved, my wife and I,
To a house of our own, I've taken them out.
Until we can find another spare drawer
They're packed in a cardboard box in the hall.

So this dead, middle-aged, middle-class man
Killed by a misfired shell, and his wife
Dead of cirrhosis, have left one son
Aged nine, aged nineteen, aged twenty-six,
Who has buried them both in a cardboard box.

GEORGE MACBETH

George MacBeth writes:

Imagination can be stimulated by any of the senses. Poets tend often to be visual or auditory, or affected by taste or smell. Schiller found it helpful when composing to sniff a drawer full of rotten apples, while Housman enjoyed a preliminary half of bitter. My own imagination is primarily a tactile or touch one, and poems come from physical contact with material objects. These can be exotic, like Japanese swords which I collect; or they can be everyday things which are emotionally loaded. In particular, I find that objects which belonged to my parents have great power over my will to write.

My father was killed in the Second World War when I was nine and my mother died of a liver disease when I was nineteen. The things my father had in the pockets of his uniform when he was hit by a shell, and the things my mother had in the bedside cabinet at the hospital where she died, have lain together in a drawer for over thirty years. Whenever I take them out, or touch them, I renew, sometimes in great strength, the emotions of guilt and grief I feel about their deaths, and perhaps the sense of pride I have in the memory of their being.

These are tangled and heady feelings and I believe that the objects – a crocodile handbag, a khaki lanyard, a powder compact – serve to anchor their pull. Without some direct hold on the reality of the past, I would incline to find it a cloudy and mesmerising place. As it is, the expended lives of my parents remain solid and available. I have some access to them through the echoing presence of their belongings.

I wrote *The Drawer* when I was twenty-six. Three dates – the two death dates and my age at the point of composition – form the second to last line of the poem. I hope they give it something of the formal exactness of a tombstone. The poem strives to avoid any metaphor or comparison: I wanted the things to speak for themselves. There is a rhythm, with a regular four-stroke beat per line, but rhyme is avoided. Only the feeling, encapsulated in the objects, and offered in honour of the dead, is encouraged to remain.

Of course, you may find the poem too drab for your taste. Not all poems appeal to all readers. But *The Drawer*, if you do like it, may offer some ideas for work of your own. Do you have mementoes of an absent sister, or a girl friend, or a remembered holiday; a lock of hair, a scented scarf or a handful of pebbles? Poets with tactile imaginations can use such material.

We live in an age of 'as if'. Aristotle, the great Greek critic, said that metaphor was the heart of poetry. Many modern critics and poets seem to agree with him. Some admired modern names have made careers out of apt comparison. But there may be times when a comparison becomes an evasion, when a metaphor is an excuse for showing off. It takes hard work and skill to think out exactly what something is like and to put it in words. But it also takes hard work and skill to see things exactly as they are and to put this plainly without colour or tricks.

☐ George Macbeth makes some useful suggestions for your own writing. As in his own poem, try and write without using metaphors or other similes – try and write about your object, and your feelings about it, exactly as it is 'without colour or tricks'.

☐ It can be interesting to write about an object you have not seen before. Hold it in your hands and feel its weight and texture. Try and guess its history.

ANTHOLOGY 6: George MacBeth

A Child's Garden

Who was here. Before his cat
Washed and rose. Without his shoes
Who inched outside while someone's hat
Made a noise. Light feet helped. Who's.

Whose are these eggs? Ladybird's.
Hard like crumbs of sleep. She flies
Off to help who find some words
For sounds and things. Who's two puffed eyes

Tug at flowers now for bees
Tucked away. Some try to hide
In pouting fox-gloves' jugs. Who sees
Their fat bears' thighs, though, wedged inside

Scouring honey. Look! Rare stones
In lupin leaves. Who's flapping gown
Shakes them all out. Ow! Who's bones
Aren't awake, make who fall down

Biting earth. Who hears a sound.
Whose are these wet softish hairs
Brushing someone's mouth? Can bound
As quick as you. Whoosh! Peter scares

A thin bird. Zip! Squawk! Its beak
Almost nipped who's fattest worm
Head and tail. Who hears him squeak
Through the grass. Who sees him squirm

Down a hole. Who wants to kiss
His frightened worm. Who's coolish knees
Push him up to clematis
He thinks it's called. It makes him sneeze.

A Poem for Breathing

   Trudging through drifts along the hedge, we
Probe at the flecked, white essence with sticks. Across
     The hill field, mushroom-brown in
    The sun, the mass of the sheep trundle
As though on small wheels. With a jerk, the farmer

   Speaks, quietly pleased. *Here's one*. And we
Hunch round while he digs. Dry snow flies like caster
     Sugar from the jabbing edge
    Of the spade. The head rubs clear first, a
Yellow cone with eyes. The farmer leans, panting,

   On the haft. *Will you grab him from the
Front?* I reach down, grope for greasy fur, rough, neat
     Ears. I grip at shoulders, while
    He heaves at the coarse, hairy
Backside. With a clumsy lug, it's up, scrambling

For a hold on the white, soft grass. It
Stares round, astonished to be alive. Then it
	Runs, like a rug on legs, to
	Join the shy others. Ten dark little
Pellets of dung steam in the hole, where it lay

	Dumped, and sank in. *You have to probe with*
The pole along the line of the rest of the
	Hedge. They tend to be close. We
	Probe, floundering in Wellingtons, breath
Rasping hard in the cold. The released one is

	All right. He has found his pen in the
Sun. I dig in the spade's thin haft, close to barbed
	Wire. Someone else speaks. *Here's*
	Another. And it starts again. The
Rush to see, the leaning sense of hush, and the

	Snow-flutter as we grasp for the quick
Life buried in the ivory ground. *There were*
	Ninety-eight, and I counted
	Ninety-five. That means one more. And I
Kneel to my spade, feeling the chill seep through my

	Boots. The sun burns dark. I imagine
The cold-worn ears, the legs bunched in the foetus
	Position for warmth. I smell
	The feathery, stale white duvet, the
Hot air from the nostrils, burning upwards. And

	I crouch above the sheep, hunched in its
Briar bunk below the hedge. From the field, it
	Hears the bleat of its friends, their
	Far joy. It feels only the cushions
Of frost on its frozen back. I breathe, slowly,

	Trying to melt that hard-packed snow. I
Breathe, melting a little snow with my breath. If
	Everyone in the whole
	World would breathe here, it might help. Breathe
Here a little, as you read, it might still help.

George MacBeth writes:

Writing courses at the Arvon Foundation's house in Devon, Totleigh
Barton, often encourage the tutors themselves to turn out new work.
Sometimes an unusual event may produce two poems on the same
subject. This happened when I shared the teaching of a winter poetry
course with Wes Magee.

For two days, after a heavy snowfall, we were cut off in the house
and unable to get cars started or up the hill. A local farmer, needing
help to dig out sheep which were buried in snowdrifts, asked some of
us if we'd be willing to give a hand, and we agreed.

The sheep tend to be buried near to the line of a hedge, as the
drifts here are often deepest, and the sheep have sought shelter from
the wind under the branches. The way to find them when there is no
surface sign of their presence was quickly shown to us. What you do
is to start at one corner and measure out a distance slightly less than
the average sheep. Then you take a stride forward and thrust a long
pole into the snow as far as you can until you strike hard earth. You
then repeat the process with similar strides until, perhaps, one time
the pole stops at something soft, and yet flexible.

It may be a sheep! You dig down with a spade and, if you're lucky,
you may be rewarded by a pair of anxious eyes staring up at you
from a triangular skull. This did indeed happen to one of us and both
Wes and I were so struck by the experience that we independently
wrote poems about it. Mine, rather longer than his, is very much a
recording of the event in a plain, fairly prosaic style. But it takes off at
the end into a wider realm, speculating about the place of caring in
the world.

Of course, I know that you can't literally help find buried sheep
under snow by breathing, but the idea of feeling pity as you breathe
is a symbolic one. I try to bring out the sense of a steady breathing as
I read the poem aloud.

Owl

is my favourite. Who flies
like a nothing through the night,
who-whoing. Is a feather
duster in leafy corners ring-a-rosy-ing
boles of mice. Twice

you hear him call. Who
is he looking for? You hear
him hoovering over the floor
of the wood. O would you be gold
rings in the driving skull

if you could? Hooded and
vulnerable by the winter suns
owl looks. Is the grain of bark
in the dark. Round beaks are at
work in the pellety nest,

resting. Owl is an eye
in the barn. For a hole
in the trunk owl's blood
is to blame. Black talons in the
petrified fur! Cold walnut hands

on the case of the brain! In the reign
of the chicken owl comes like
a god. Is a goad in
the rain to the pink eyes,
dripping. For a meal in the day

flew, killed, on the moor. Six
mouths are the seed of his
arc in the season. Torn meat
from the sky. Owl lives
by the claws of his brain. On the branch

in the sever of the hand's
twigs owl is a backward look.
Flown wind in the skin. Fine
rain in the bones. Owl breaks
like the day. Am an owl, am an owl.

The Compasses

Baroque-handled and sharp
With blunt lead in their lips
And their fluted legs together
My father's compasses
Lie buried in this flat box.

I take it out of its drawer,
Snap old elastic bands
And rub the frayed leatherette:
It smells faintly of smoke:
The broken hinges yawn.

As I level the case to look
A yellowed protractor claps
Against black-papered board,
Sliding loose in the lid
Behind a torn silk flap.

I look in the base at the dusty
Velvet cavities:
Dead-still, stiff in the joints
And side by side they lie
Like armoured knights on a tomb.

One by one I lift
Them out in the winter air
And wipe some dust away:
Screw back their gaping lips
And bend the rigid knees.

In an inch of hollowed bone
Two cylinders of lead
Slither against each other
With a faint scurrying sound.
I lay them carefully back

And close the case. In Crookes
My father's bones are scattered
In a measured space of ground:
Given his flair for drawing
These compasses should be there

Not locked away in a box
By an uninstructed son
But like an Egyptian king's
Ready shield and swords
Beside his crumbling hand.

The Day the World Ended

FOR JOHN BETJEMAN

The washing machine was whirling away,
    The cat was licking its tail,
A pile of clothes was on top and done,
    And a pile was below in a pail.

The basement was growing steamy and warm,
    The cat was alert and wise,
The dryer was doing its job quite well,
    And the jeans were rattling their flies.

The regular wash was all clean and dry,
    The *Tide* was back on the sink,
The handkerchiefs were all fresh and smooth,
    And the towels looked bright and pink.

The revolving drum had come to a halt,
    The shirts were all shut inside,
The air was thick with the smell of suds,
    And the cat's eyes were open wide.

The world was travelling round the sun,
    The moon was out in the West,
A spider was tottering over the floor,
    And the maid was wringing a vest.

The hangers were on the clothes horse,
    The socks were dripping and wet,
The cat had gone for a plate of fish,
    And the sun had started to set.

The light was up in the living-room,
    The lamp was down in the hall,
The cat was hunting a brown rat,
    And nothing had happened at all.

One Gone, Eight to Go

On a night of savage frost,
This year, my smallest cat,
The fluffy one, got lost.
And I thought that that was that.

Until, late home, I heard,
As I fumbled for my key,
The weak sound of some bird.
He was there, mewing to me.

There, on the icy sill,
Lifting his crusted head,
He looked far worse than ill.
He looked, I'd say, quite dead.

Indoors, though, he could eat,
As he showed, and fluffed his tail.
So much for a plate of meat.
So much for a storm of hail.

Now, by the burning grate,
I stroke his fragile spine,
Thinking of time, and fate.
Lives go. Men don't have nine,

As kittens do, to waste.
This lucky one survives,
And purrs, affronted-faced.
But even he, who thrives

Tonight, in my cupped hands,
And will grow big and grey,
Will sense, in time, the sands,
And fail, and shrink away.